Outdoor Adventures
KAYAKING

James De Medeiros

WEIGL PUBLISHERS INC

Published by Weigl Publishers Inc.
350 5th Avenue, Suite 3304, PMB 6G
New York, NY 10118-0069

Website: www.weigl.com

Library of Congress Cataloging-in-Publication Data

De Medeiros, James.
  Kayaking / James De Medeiros.
     p. cm. -- (Outdoor adventures)
  Includes index.
  ISBN-13: 978-1-59036-663-9 (hard cover : alk. paper)
  ISBN-13: 978-1-59036-664-6 (soft cover : alk. paper)
  1. Kayaking--Juvenile literature. I. Title.
  GV784.3.D4 2008
  797.122'4--dc22
                                        2006101978

Printed in the United States of America
1 2 3 4 5 6 7 8 9 0 11 10 09 08 07

Every reasonable effort has been made to trace ownership and to obtain permission to reprint
copyright material. The publishers would be pleased to have any errors or omissions brought to their
attention so that they may be corrected in subsequent printings.

Project Coordinator
Tatiana Tomljanoivc

Design
Terry Paulhus

All of the Internet URLs given in the book were valid at the time of
publication. However, due to the dynamic nature of the Internet, some
addresses may have changed, or sites may have ceased to exist since
publication. While the author and publisher regret any inconvenience
this may cause readers, no responsibility for any such changes can be
accepted by either the author or the publisher.

CONTENTS

All About Kayaking

A kayak is a small, light boat. It has a single opening in the center called a cockpit. Kayakers sit inside the cockpit. Kayakers can move and steer the kayak with a double-bladed paddle.

The Inuit made the first kayaks from wooden frames and animal skins. They had two types of kayaks. One was wide and had space to store items. The other kayak was long and sleek. The shape of this kayak helped the kayaker move more quickly through the water.

Over time, the design of the kayak changed. Different materials were used to make kayaks. **Synthetic** material replaced animal skins. In the 1950s, **fiberglass** started to be used instead of wooden frames. In the 1980s, fiberglass frames were replaced by plastic frames. All of these changes were made to improve kayaking as a sport.

Competitive kayaking began in 1873. That year, the Canoe Club began holding kayak races. Today, many people around the world enjoy kayaking for fun and for sport.

Kayaking is one way to view the icebergs in Alaska.

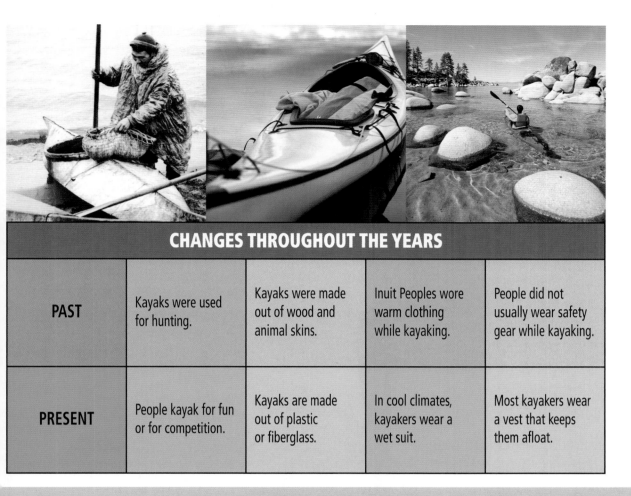

CHANGES THROUGHOUT THE YEARS

PAST	Kayaks were used for hunting.	Kayaks were made out of wood and animal skins.	Inuit Peoples wore warm clothing while kayaking.	People did not usually wear safety gear while kayaking.
PRESENT	People kayak for fun or for competition.	Kayaks are made out of plastic or fiberglass.	In cool climates, kayakers wear a wet suit.	Most kayakers wear a vest that keeps them afloat.

Paddling through whitewaters can be challenging. It also can be dangerous.

Getting Started

Kayaking can be a dangerous sport. It is important to be prepared with the proper equipment, including safety gear. One of the most important pieces of equipment is the kayak. There are many different types of kayaks, such as touring kayaks, folding kayaks, inflatable kayaks, and rigid kayaks.

Folding kayaks are similar to Inuit kayaks. They are made by placing fabric over a light wooden or aluminum frame. Folding kayaks can be taken apart and folded for storage. They are as sturdy as regular kayaks.

Touring kayaks are used for long-distance trips or for kayaking at sea. They are larger than many other types of kayaks. This makes them less likely to tip or turn over. Touring kayaks are made from plastic or fiberglass. They may have a place to store equipment.

Inflatable kayaks float better than many other types of kayaks. They are less likely to tip over. This is because they are filled with air. When not in use, the air can be removed from an inflatable kayak.

The most common type of kayak is the rigid kayak.

All the Right Equipment

Most experienced kayakers want their kayak to have a tight cockpit space. Beginners learn better with a bigger cockpit. There are also multiple passenger kayaks that are best for families who like to kayak together. It is important to have storage space on board the kayak.

Double-bladed kayak paddles come in different lengths and widths. A long paddle is good for a long kayak or tall person. A shorter paddle is good for a shorter kayak or person.

A skirt is a piece of fabric that fits around a kayaker's waist. It attaches to the edge of the cockpit. Skirts prevent water from filling the kayak and causing it to sink.

Wet suits keep kayakers warm in cold water. A wet suit absorbs water. A kayaker's body heat warms up the water that the wet suit absorbs. This creates a warm layer between the kayaker and the cold.

A personal flotation device is a jacket or vest the kayaker wears in the water to keep afloat.

A helmet will protect a kayaker from hitting his or her head on objects in the water, such as rocks and logs.

Kayaking Basics

There are many ways to paddle a kayak. As a beginner, the most important techniques are the forward, sweep, and brace strokes. The forward stroke helps the kayaker move forward. The kayaker places the right side of the paddle in the water near the front of the kayak. He or she pulls the blade toward the back of the boat. Then, the kayaker places the left side of the paddle in the water and pulls back.

Sweep strokes can turn the kayak forward or backward. This is done by placing the paddle in the water near the front of the kayak. Then, the kayaker sweeps the paddle out to the side and back, forming an arc in the water.

Brace strokes are especially important for beginners. Bracing keeps kayaks from tipping over. The simplest form of bracing keeps one blade of the paddle under water. High and low bracing requires kayakers to push the blade of their paddle against the flow of water. This is done by leaning forward.

Kayaking with friends is a good way to experience nature.

Even if a kayaker knows how to brace, kayaks can still tip over, leaving kayakers upside down. To turn the kayak right side up, kayakers must be able to roll their kayak. The roll is achieved when kayakers, still in the kayak, move their hips so that their bodies are twisted sideways. At this point, they lift their paddles out of the water, keeping them **parallel** to the kayak. Then, they sweep the right paddle blades away from the kayak and into the water. The left elbow should be kept close to the body. Kayakers snap their hips back into a straight position while sweeping, turning their kayak right side up.

get CONNECTED

To learn advanced kayaking moves, such as the whippet, visit http://gorp.away.com. Enter "kayaking moves" into the search engine.

Rolling a kayak takes strength, skill, and experience. This is an important skill to know before kayaking in challenging waters.

Kayaking Levels

Whitewater, or river, kayaking is an **extreme sport**. It requires skill and experience. There are six levels, or classes, of difficulty for this sport. Beginners often start in the first two classes. The first class is the easiest. At this level, the water moves quickly but without any waves or **obstructions**. If the kayak rolls or tips and the kayaker falls out, the water is mild. It is easy to swim to shore. Class two is similar to class one, but there may be rocks in the water and slightly bigger waves.

The third class is for experienced kayakers. It has big waves and narrow paths. The fourth class has powerful waves that make paddling more difficult. Inexperienced kayakers should avoid these conditions.

Class five is extremely difficult and is for experts only. Rescues are difficult to perform on class five or higher **rapids**. These routes are known for violent and obstructed paths with extremely fast-flowing water.

It is a good idea to take a boating and water safety course before attempting to kayak.

get CONNECTED

Try navigating a virtual kayak down a river through this online game http://gamescene.com/River_Kayak_game.html.

Rapids can change in difficulty during different seasons. It is important to check the conditions of rapids each time before going kayaking.

Class six is known for extremely dangerous conditions. It is strongly advised to avoid class six rapids. They are dangerous and highly unpredictable. Even expert kayakers risk seriously hurting themselves by trying class six rapids.

RIVER KAYAKING CLASSES OF DIFFICULTY	
CLASS 1	no waves or obstructions
CLASS 2	small rocks, slightly bigger waves
CLASS 3	narrow paths, bigger waves
CLASS 4	difficult, powerful waves
CLASS 5	violent and obstructed fast-flowing waters
CLASS 6	extremely dangerous conditions

Staying Safe

Kayaking can be dangerous because it is hard to predict what might happen in the rapids. With proper training and experience, most people learn to read the signs of dangerous rapids so they can plan fun, safe trips.

To stay safe, kayakers must remain calm. They should always know their skill level and not attempt to do anything beyond that level. Kayakers who have never paddled for more than two hours at one time should not go on a four-hour trip. Kayakers cannot take breaks on the water. The only time kayakers can rest is when they have returned to shore.

One of the most important skills in kayaking is the ability to judge the danger of rapids.

Kayakers should always check weather reports before going on a trip. It is dangerous to kayak during a storm. Waves and wind can change a class three rapid to a class six. Another risk is extreme cold. Cool temperatures and wet clothing increase the chance of a kayaker getting **hypothermia**.

All kayakers should learn rescue skills. Accidents can happen at any time, and kayakers always need to be prepared to help another kayaker or themselves. Rescue skills include **cardiopulmonary resuscitation** (CPR) and basic first aid. Kayakers should also know kayaking signals, such as stop, help, or all is clear. To signal stop, kayakers stretch both arms out from their sides to form a horizontal line. Help is signaled by waving a helmet, life vest, or paddle above the kayaker's head. To let others know all is clear ahead, kayakers hold one arm or a paddle straight up, high above their heads.

TIP

Treat hypothermia by removing all wet clothing. Put on warm, dry clothing. Cut a hole for your head in a garbage bag, and wear the bag like a shirt. This will help stop heat loss.

Try matching the following rescue signals.

1   2   3

A) Stop   B) Help   C) All is clear or move forward

Other Outdoor Adventures

There are many outdoor activities that can be enjoyed on the water in addition to kayaking. Some of these activities include whitewater rafting, water skiing, fishing, and canoeing.

Whitewater Rafting

In whitewater rafting, people shoot down river rapids. The rafts are inflatable, rubber boats. Often, they are steered by a professional guide who sits in the back of the raft. Many people can fit in a raft. They help the guide steer the raft.

Water Skiing

Water skiing was invented in 1922 by an 18-year-old boy named Ralph Samuelson. To water ski, the skiier is pulled behind a boat. People who become good at water skiing can take part in competitions that are held around the world.

Fishing

Beneath the surface of rivers, lakes, and oceans lie many types of life, including fish. **Recreational** fishers use a fishing rod, line, hook, and **bait** to catch fish. Fishing can be done from the shore or from a boat or kayak. Most types of fishing are not physically demanding. People of any fitness level can fish. However, fishers do need patience to enjoy this pastime.

get CONNECTED

To learn more about fishing, check out www.takemefishing.org.

Canoeing

A canoe looks like a kayak. However, a canoe does not have a skirt. Most canoes are built to fit more than one person. Canoe paddles have a blade at one end. Canoeing is done on calm waters with few or small waves. It is a good way to travel rivers and lakes with a group of people and enjoy the outdoor scenery.

Kayaking Around the World

EVERGLADES NATIONAL PARK, UNITED STATES

The Everglades in Florida have become famous for their variety of wildlife. There are more than 300 species of birds here. The Everglades are also known to be the only place in the world where alligators and crocodiles live together in nature. Although kayakers need to be careful to avoid dangerous wildlife, the Everglades offer spectacular scenery for the adventurous.

NORTH AMERICA

ATLANTIC OCEAN

PACIFIC OCEAN

SOUTH AMERICA

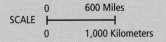

SCALE
0 — 600 Miles
0 — 1,000 Kilometers

N
W — E
S

There are many places in the world where people can kayak. The best places to kayak depend on what a kayaker enjoys the most. Some places have challenging class six rapids. Others have beautiful natural areas. The following are a few of the places to kayak around the world.

ARCTIC OCEAN

ARCTIC OCEAN

CYCLADES ISLANDS, GREECE

The Cyclades Islands in Greece are made up of more than 30 islands, including Delos, Mykonos, Paros, Naxos, Tinos, and Santorini. There are many beautiful beaches in the Cyclades Islands. Kayakers can enjoy the warm climate while paddling and try to spot sea life in the clear water.

ASIA

EUROPE

ROCK ISLANDS, PALAU

The Rock Islands are part of the 350 Micronesian islands in Palau. Kayakers and sport divers enjoy the area's scenery and history. The islands are famous for having sea caves, sunken ships, and even airplanes. The sunken planes in this area are from battles between Japan and the United States during World War II.

PACIFIC OCEAN

AFRICA

INDIAN OCEAN

GREAT BARRIER REEF, AUSTRALIA

The Great Barrier Reef is located off the coast of Queensland, Australia. It is the largest coral reef in the world. It is home to rare sea life. In total, there are about 4,000 types of **mollusks**, 1,500 types of fish, 16 types of sea snakes, and 215 types of birds. Kayakers can enjoy viewing a unique environment. However, they must be careful not to damage the **ecosystem**.

AUSTRALIA

Join the Club

There are many kayaking clubs all over the world. No matter where a person lives, chances are good that there is a kayaking club nearby. The U.S. state of California alone has more than 15 kayaking clubs.

Competitive kayaking is becoming more popular around the world. At the Summer Olympic Games, there are kayaking competitions for both men and women. The events include whitewater and flat water races. The racers with the fastest times win the competitions and the medals for their countries.

Kayaking has been an Olympic sport since 1936.

Many smaller competitions take place throughout the world as well. It is at these local events that kayakers sharpen their skills. These competitions help decide which kayakers will represent their countries at the Olympic Games and world championships.

SEE Kayaks – A sea kayak links directory

http://www.seekayak.com/

Google

World Atlas – MSN Encarta   Welcome to Weigl   Orisinal : M...ing Sunshine   RBC Royal Bank Gateway

SEE Kayak

SEE Kayaks - Sea Kayaking Directory

Kayak Reviews
Top Kayaks of the year! Compare by price & performance.
Outside.away.com

Kayak.com
Your Official Travel Site. One Search for Low Rental Rates
www.Kayak.com

13 Great Sea Kayak Trips
Outstanding guided trips in Canada, Greenland and Baja, Mexico
www.blackfeather.com

Maui's Kayak Fun
Exceptional Eco Tours Snorkel Pristine Coral Reefs
www.southpacifickayaks.com

Ads by Goooooogle   Advertise on this site

| Home | Add a Link | Modify a Link | What's New | Top Rated | Email Updates | Random Link | Search |

SEE Kayaks is the largest directory of sea kayaking related web sites. It contains the most links to sea kayaking related sites on the web, with 1825 unique pages currently listed and new sea kayaking pages being added almost every day. If you can not find your favorite site in this directory, please feel free to add a link to your kayaking related web page.

If you are looking for a place to talk about sea kayaking, head over to the Sea Kayak Forum for online discussions about sea kayak trips, sea kayak techniques, kayak construction, and canoe and kayak design.

This site is sponsored by Guillemot Kayaks, designer of high performance sea kayaks.

Categories:

Businesses (1112) new
Sea kayak businesses. Manufacturers, Retail, Rental, Guides, Designers. Kits and plans.

Clubs and Associations (230)
Sea kayaking clubs, water trail associations,

Indices (49)
Other directories and indexes information related to se

Publications (29) new
Magazines and e-zi kayaking. Books ar

Reference Resource
Informational resource

Healthy Habits

Kayakers must stay fit. One of the best ways to keep in shape is to eat healthy foods. Balanced meals of grains, fruits, vegetables, dairy products, and protein will give kayakers more energy.

Grains include anything made from wheat or rice, such as bread, cereal, and pasta. All fruits and vegetables are healthy. Most nutritionists recommend eating five to ten servings of fruits or vegetables a day. A serving can be half a cup of juice or a piece of medium-sized fruit, such as a banana. People should choose low-fat dairy products, such as skim milk, low-fat cheese, or yogurt. They need to include lean meats, such as fish or chicken in their diet.

Eating cereal with skim milk and fruit is a good way to get the necessary nutrition needed by people who kayak.

Kayakers need energy, flexibility, and strength to paddle. Whether people want to be competitive or recreational kayakers, the more strength they have, the easier the activity will be. Flexibility allows kayakers to twist their upper body. Twisting is an essential movement for the sport. Kayakers must be able to twist to perform rolls and flip upside down kayaks right side up.

DRY LAND STRETCHES

These exercises stretch the body in the three directions a person can move in a kayak. Try holding each of them for 15 to 20 seconds, and repeat three times on each side.

"C" STRETCH
Sit on the floor, and raise arms above head. Lean to the side.

TORSO TWIST
Sitting down, twist chest and shoulders while keeping lower half still.

LEG STRETCH
Lie on back, lifting one leg straight up in the air. Grasp leg with hands and pull.

Stretching before kayaking can help prevent injuries.

Brain Teasers

Test your kayaking knowledge by trying to answer these brain teasers.

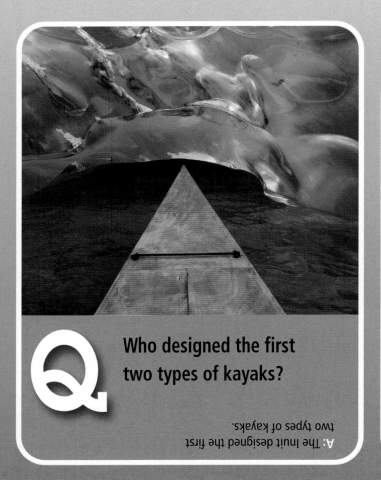

Q Who designed the first two types of kayaks?

A: The Inuit designed the first two types of kayaks.

Q What year did kayaking become an Olympic sport?

A: Kayaking became an Olympic sport in 1936.

Q What are the main three kayaking strokes?

A: The three main kayaking strokes are the forward, sweep, and brace strokes.

Q Where does a kayaker sit?

A: The kayaker sits in the middle of the boat in an area called the cockpit.

Q What piece of equipment is used to steer the kayak?

A: The paddle is used by the kayaker to move the kayak in any direction.

Q How many classes of rapids are there?

A: There are six classes of rapids.

Glossary

bait: food put on a hook to attract fish

cardiopulmonary resuscitation: a life-saving technique that combines rescue breathing with chest compressions; used when a person stops breathing and his or her heart stops beating

ecosystem: all the living and non-living things in a certain area

extreme sport: difficult or dangerous physical activity

fiberglass: a strong material made from fine threads of glass

hypothermia: a dangerous loss of body heat caused by extremely cold weather

mollusks: sea creatures, such as clams, squid, octopuses, and oysters

obstructions: objects in the water that a kayaker might hit, such as rocks and tree branches

parallel: being the same distance apart at all points

rapids: shallow parts of rivers where rocks are exposed and fast-moving water creates waves

recreational: something done for fun or relaxation, such as hobbies, games, and sports

synthetic: made by people; not natural

Index